Nuclear Submariners

By Antony Loveless

CRABTREE
Publishing Company
www.crabtreebooks.com

The World's MOST DANGEROUS Jobs

Editors: Mark Sachner, Adrianna Morganelli
Editorial director: Kathy Middleton
Proofreader: Redbud Editorial
Production coordinator: Margaret Salter
Prepress technician: Margaret Salter
Project director: Ruth Owen
Designer: Elaine Wilkinson
Cover design: Alix Wood

Photo credits:
Corbis: Steve Kaufman: page 24; Roger Ressmeyer: page 25
Department of Defense: cover (top), pages 4, 6, 7, 11, 13,
    18–19, 21, 22, 27, 28
Getty Images: Royal Navy: page 9
Antony Loveless: cover (bottom); pages 1, 5, 14, 17
Shutterstock: page 16

COVER STORY

◄ **COVER (top) – The United States Navy (USN) fast attack submarine USS _Norfolk_ surfaces in the Arabian Sea.**

◄ **COVER (bottom) – An XO (Executive Officer) looks through a submarine's periscope.**

PAGE 1 – A navigation officer studies a chart which shows the position of shipwrecks on the submarine's route, Iraq.

Library and Archives Canada Cataloguing in Publication

Loveless, Antony
    Nuclear submariners / Antony Loveless.

(The world's most dangerous jobs)
Includes index.
ISBN 978-0-7787-5097-0 (bound).--ISBN 978-0-7787-5111-3 (pbk.)

    1. Submariners--Juvenile literature. 2. Nuclear submarines--Juvenile
literature. I. Title. II. Series: World's most dangerous jobs

V857.5.L69 2009   j623.825'74   C2009-903383-6

Library of Congress Cataloging-in-Publication Data

Loveless, Antony.
    Nuclear submariners / Antony Loveless.
        p. cm. -- (The world's most dangerous jobs)
    Includes index.
    ISBN 978-0-7787-5111-3 (pbk. : alk. paper) -- ISBN 978-0-7787-5097-0
(reinforced library binding : alk. paper)
    1. Nuclear submarines--Juvenile literature. 2. Submariners--Juvenile
literature. I. Title.

V857.5.L68 2010
359.9'3834--dc22

2009022422

Published by CRABTREE PUBLISHING COMPANY in 2010

Published in Canada
Crabtree Publishing
616 Welland Ave.
St. Catharines, ON
L2M 5V6

Published in the United States
Crabtree Publishing
PMB16A
350 Fifth Ave., Suite 3308
New York, NY 10118

Published in the United Kingdom
Crabtree Publishing
Lorna House, Suite 3.03, Lorna Road
Hove, East Sussex, UK
BN3 3EL

Published in Australia
Crabtree Publishing
386 Mt. Alexander Rd.
Ascot Vale (Melbourne)
VIC 3032

CONTENTS

LIFE BENEATH THE OCEAN

In today's world, most people are unlikely to take part in dangerous activities during their day at work. They sit at desks in offices, or they work in shops and factories.

▲ The United States Navy (USN) fast attack submarine USS *Norfolk* surfaces in the Arabian Sea.

For some people, however, living with danger is very much a part of their everyday life.

Nuclear submariners do their job 1,000 feet (300 meters) below the surface of the ocean. They spend up to six months at a time at sea and rarely surface. Crew members live in a pressurized metal tube.

They work within a few feet of one of the most lethal substances known to humankind—**radioactive** nuclear material.

Nuclear submarines are the main striking power of the navy fleet. Some submarines can fire **ballistic missiles** onto shore-based targets. Others are attack submarines. They are designed to fire **torpedoes** at enemy submarines and ships.

Attack submarines can shadow an enemy vessel for long periods of time. They move silently and at high speed. Inside the submarine, the crew is ready to attack with deadly effectiveness when the time is right.

"In wartime, our role is to hunt enemy submarines and destroy them— before we can be hunted down."

John, United States Navy (USN) Submariner

▼ Royal Navy shore-based crewmen peer into the opened hatch of the U.K.'s HMS *Trenchant*. For the crew inside, it is their first sight of sky, and a breath of fresh air for three months.

A nuclear submarine is powered by its own nuclear reactor. The reactor generates large amounts of energy to power the ship. Nuclear submarines never need to be refueled throughout their working lives.

THE SUBMARINES

Attack submarines are known as SSNs (Ship Submersible Nuclears). They are often called "fast attack submarines." Their role is to pursue and attack enemy submarines and surface ships using torpedoes.

SSNs also carry **cruise missiles**. These weapons can be fitted with high-explosive warheads to attack enemy targets on shore.

SSNs conduct intelligence, surveillance, and reconnaissance missions. This means they gather information on enemy activities and secretly follow enemy submarines and ships. Sometimes the submarines lay **mines** at sea. The mines float just below the water's surface.

SSBNs (Ship Submersible Ballistic Nuclears) carry long-range ballistic missiles with nuclear warheads. These weapons are designed to be fired from the submarine onto land.

Nuclear weapons are often described as a nation's "nuclear deterrent." These weapons are so powerful they could bring about the end of the world. This fact actually stops nations from using nuclear weapons against each other.

◄ The United States Navy (USN) SSBN submarine USS *Florida.* Submariners can be seen on deck.

▼ A navy SEAL (Sea Air and Land forces) practices leaving a submarine during a training exercise. A navy diver films the training mission.

SSNs take part in special operations—for example, inserting Special Forces into enemy territory. The submarine surfaces to a shallow depth, and Special Forces soldiers climb from the hatch and swim ashore under the cover of darkness.

THE DANGERS

Life onboard a nuclear submarine is highly organized and often quiet. Danger is a part of everyday life, even when not at war.

Submariners rely on many different systems to deliver their air and water. If any of these vital systems fail, the lives of the crew may be in danger.

In 2007, breathing equipment failed onboard the United Kingdom's Royal Navy submarine HMS *Tireless*. At the time, the submarine was deep below the ice at the North Pole. Two submariners were killed.

If a submarine collides with something under water, or there is an accident onboard, the crew may not be able to escape.

In August 2000, 118 men died onboard the Russian nuclear submarine *Kursk*. The fuel in a torpedo ignited, starting a fire. The fire caused torpedoes to detonate inside the submarine. Explosions ripped through the ship, causing it to sink to the ocean floor.

Many of the Russian submariners were still alive when the *Kursk* sank. Russian, Norwegian, and British rescuers tried to reach the men for several days. When rescue divers finally entered the submarine, the men were all dead.

▶ The crew of this LR5 rescue submarine prepares for the *Kursk* rescue. The submarine is traveling to the accident aboard the *Normand Pioneer*.

A British LR5 rescue submarine was sent to help the Kursk. The LR5 is designed to connect to a submarine's escape hatch. The submariners climb into the LR5 and are taken to the surface 15 at a time.

LIMITED OPTIONS

Submarines normally operate at depths greater than 600 feet (180 m) below the surface. At this depth, options for escape are very limited.

A rescue can be tried using a small deepwater submersible (mini-submarine), such as the LR5. The rescue submarine can carry about 15 people at a time. Many trips would be needed, to rescue a typical crew of 150. In that time, a damaged submarine might flood, or the crew might run out of air if the breathing equipment has failed.

If a submarine is less than 600 feet (180 m) below the surface, submariners are trained to escape without help from outside.

The latest U.K. and U.S. submarines carry Submarine Escape Immersion Equipment (SEIE) MK-10 whole-body escape suits. The crew is able to leave the submarine through the escape hatch at a rate of about eight per hour. There is no breathing equipment in the suits. The crew members simply leave the escape hatch and push for the surface.

Most submariners take it for granted, that if an accident happens at a great depth, there will be no escape. Therefore, submariners live and work by very strict rules to ensure the safety of everyone onboard.

MK-10 escape suits keep the crew members warm and contain built-in, one-person life rafts that can be inflated when they reach the surface.

▲ A submariner from the SSN USS *Key West* receives training in using the MK-10 escape suit.

SUBMARINER TRAINING

Life onboard a submarine is not to everyone's liking. That's why every member of the submarine force is a volunteer. Trainees join the navy and then volunteer for submarine service.

There are several tests that volunteers must take to assess if they are suitable to be a submariner. The tests determine how well the volunteers can solve problems. They also show how good they are at English and math and whether they understand mechanics.

Volunteers who perform well on the tests advance to training school. Basic training includes teamwork, discipline, firefighting, first aid, and weapons skills. Basic training is followed by specialist training in warfare, weapons, working with nuclear power, and escape training. After their shore-based training, submariners gain real experience by working as part of a submarine crew.

Submariners are some of the most highly skilled people in the navy. They can choose their own area of specialization, but each one must be able to operate, maintain, and repair every system or piece of equipment onboard the submarine.

▼ Submariners who are "qualified in submarines" earn the right to wear silver or gold dolphins on their uniforms. In the U.S. Navy, crew members wear silver dolphins and the officers wear gold dolphins. Here, a submariner receives his gold dolphins during a "pinning ceremony."

"I was about seven years old when I saw the movie 'Crimson Tide,' and that was it for me. I wanted to be a submariner! "

Karl, Royal Navy Submariner

The periscope is the submarine's "eyes" on the world above. It is usually used by the Captain or the XO (the Executive Officer, the captain's second-in-command). The submarine comes to just below the water's surface, and the periscope extends above the water.

▲ An XO looks through a submarine's periscope. A camera can be attached to the periscope's viewfinder to photograph enemy ships when the submarine is carrying out intelligence work.

THE CREW

The Captain is in overall command of the boat and is assisted by the XO (Executive Officer) who is second-in-command. The XO runs the submarine on a day-to-day basis. This allows the Captain to step back, think tactically, and review any situation.

Mark is an XO with the Royal Navy SSN Fleet. He explains the crew set-up aboard a submarine:

"The crew is divided into different departments. The Executive Department is responsible for many important areas of life onboard. They look after routines, discipline, cleanliness, security, and health and safety. The Executive Department is headed up by the XO.

The Engineering Department is under the supervision of the Chief Engineer. They are responsible for the safe operation of the submarine's nuclear reactor.

The Weapons Department is managed by the Weapons Officer. This department maintains the ship's torpedoes, cruise missiles, and nuclear missiles. They also operate the sonar equipment which allows the ship to navigate and detect objects under the water.

The Operations Department is managed by the Navigator. This department charts the ship's position and route. They also operate the communication equipment.

Finally, the Supply Department, led by the Supply Officer, manages the ship's stores, cooks the meals, and looks after the machinery spare parts."

TURNING WATER INTO AIR

James is a Marine Engineering Officer onboard an SSN. He explains how the sea gives submariners all the air they need to breathe—even if the submarine is submerged for months at a time.

"Air onboard the sub is produced through a process called electrolysis. This process uses seawater to make air—which is great because we have plenty of seawater!

Each tiny molecule of water is made up of two hydrogen **atoms** bonded with a single oxygen atom. Electrolysis simply breaks that bond. It separates off the oxygen atom and routes the oxygen throughout the submarine for breathing.

Breathing out expels harmful **carbon dioxide** from the body and some oxygen. The carbon dioxide is removed from the submarine with special equipment. Then the breathed-out oxygen is reused with fresh oxygen added. The hydrogen part of the seawater is compressed and ejected back into the water."

◄ Water is made up of one oxygen atom and two hydrogen atoms. Its chemical symbol is H_2O.

▲ Submariners wear breathing equipment during a fire drill. A fire will spread dangerous fumes throughout the submarine. The crew must wear face masks that deliver pure oxygen and keep the fumes out.

GOING NUCLEAR

Nuclear submarines are powered by a device called a nuclear reactor. A nuclear reactor works through a process called **nuclear fission**.

This process uses the radioactive element Uranium-235 and the basic building blocks of everything in life—atoms. When a **subatomic** particle called a neutron is fired at a Uranium-235 atom, the atom's nucleus becomes unstable and splits the atom. This releases a massive amount of energy. This process is carried out again and again in the nuclear reactor.

The energy produced is used to run a generator that makes steam using seawater that has had the salt removed from it. The steam turns the submarine's turbines (large rotary engines) and the turbines generate the power to propel the submarine and generate electricity for the submarine.

▶ The Royal Navy SSBN HMS *Vanguard*. This submarine carries up to 16 Trident D5 nuclear missiles, each carrying 12 warheads.

"Modern nuclear submarines have fuel that will last for the life of the ship—that's approximately 33 years. This means a submarine can stay operational and on the frontline defending our country for long periods of time.

Safety is always paramount on a nuclear submarine because nuclear material is highly radioactive and dangerous.

The reactor is designed with 'shielding' around it to reduce **radiation** levels. Onboard, radiation levels are very low. In fact, a submariner gets less radiation at sea than a person gets on a beach from the Sun."

Ryan, Engineering Officer, United States Navy (USN) SSN

SONAR

Submarines use large underwater listening devices called "sonar" to navigate and detect other objects under water. A submarine can often hear a ship miles away.

Sonar stands for SOund NAvigation and Ranging. It gives us virtual "eyes" under water and helps us to detect ships and other submarines.

The submarine transmits a pulse into the water. I listen for how long it takes the pulse to bounce off another object such as a submarine and return. The amount of time tells me how far away the object is.

Advanced sonar systems are designed to listen for noises from other ships and submarines. We can hear a propeller turning in the water, or a ship's engines. With experience, we can tell a ship's speed, its number of propellers, and even the exact kind of ship—just by listening to the sounds.

We also hear the natural sounds of the ocean, such as whales, dolphins, and shrimp. It's really very noisy under water if you listen carefully.

Kyle, Sonar Operator, USN SSN

Noise traces show as vertical lines on a sonar operator's screen. By hovering a cursor over each line, operators can hear the sounds produced by the target through their headsets.

▲ A U.S. Navy Petty Officer checks his sonar system during a battle drill onboard the USS *Maryland*, somewhere in the Pacific Ocean.

▼ A submariner works at the main console of the submarine's ballast control panel onboard the USS *Pennsylvania*.

DIVE!

The Eng (pronounced "Enjj") is the universal navy nickname for the Chief Engineer. Robert is an Eng onboard a U.S. Navy SSN. He explains how submarines dive and surface:

"Submarines stay on the surface by keeping large compartments, called ballast tanks, filled with air. To submerge, the submarine opens special valves at the top of the ballast tanks. When the valves open, air escapes out the top of the tanks as seawater enters the tanks from the bottom. The seawater is heavier than the air so the submarine becomes heavier and submerges. If required, submarines can dive and surface very fast.

Getting to the surface can be done by blowing to the surface and by driving to the surface. Blowing to the surface is done by blowing high-pressure air into the ballast tanks. To drive to the surface, the submarine positions its planes (its stubby "wings") to rise and the submarine ascends to the surface."

Nuclear submarines generally carry enough supplies for 90 days. Food and supplies are the only thing that limit how long a submarine can stay submerged.

LIFE ONBOARD

At sea, the typical submarine day is 18 hours long. The crew is divided into three sections. Each section is on watch for six hours and off duty for 12 hours. Under special conditions, such as "battle stations" (when the submarine is in combat or is training for combat), or when entering or leaving port, the whole crew is on watch.

> When we're off watch, we eat, relax, and attend training sessions. We also study, both for advancement examinations, and in order to become qualified to stand other watch stations.
>
> Most subs carry about 400 movies that are exchanged for newer ones in each port.
>
> There is some athletic equipment onboard. We've got an exercise bike, versa climber, rowing machines, and free weights. Some people even run marathons by running around the perimeter of the missile compartment many thousands of times!

Cody, Sonar Operator, USN SSN

◄ Each bunk has a reading light and an earphone point for plugging into the submarine's audio entertainment system.

▼ Captain Garnet C. Beard runs laps onboard the USS *Alabama.* Running 12 loops around the missile tubes equals one mile (1.6 km)!

On submarines, each crew member has a small bunk with a curtain. There is a locker for personal belongings under the mattress. Sometimes there are not enough bunks to go around. Temporary bunks are fitted on storage racks in the torpedo room.

FOOD AND WATER

A submarine draws in about 10 tons of seawater each day. It is purified for drinking, washing, and cleaning. Two tons of the water supply are used in the nuclear reactor each day.

> Onboard, the watchword with water is conservation. You use the minimum amount of water when showering. Turn the water on to wet yourself. Then turn it off. Soap yourself and shampoo. Then turn the water back on only to rinse. It's surprising how quick you get used to it.
>
> **Simon, Junior Engineer, Royal Navy SSN**

The quality of the food served onboard the submarine has a great impact on crew morale.

Submariners have four meals each day—breakfast, lunch, dinner, and midnight rations of leftovers, known as "midrats." Menus include eggs, bacon, and cereal for breakfast. The crew has sandwiches, hamburgers, and soup for lunch. For dinner there is pasta, steak, chicken, and pork dishes.

Imagine shopping for up to 150 crew members for six months and planning every meal!

▶ A United States Navy submariner prepares food in the galley onboard the USS *Norfolk*.

"There are two of us in the galley (kitchen).

The fresh fruit, vegetables, eggs, and milk don't usually last for more than a few weeks. So, we have to work wonders with canned and frozen foods. We bake fresh bread every day.

On long deployments there is not enough storage space. Cans of food are stored on the floors in the passageways throughout the boat and everyone simply walks on the top of the cans!

Aaron, Chef, Royal Navy SSN

ACTION STATIONS

Christian is the XO onboard one of the United Kingdom's SSBNs. This submarine provides the U.K.'s **nuclear deterrent** in the form of 16 Trident D5 nuclear missiles. He describes what would happen in the event of a nuclear attack on the United Kingdom.

▶ A U.S. Navy Trident II D5 missile is launched by a SSBN from below the water's surface. This is a test launch with no warheads attached to the missile.

◀ This illustration shows how Trident D5 missiles are launched from an SSBN.

In our control room, there's a safe attached to the floor with an inner safe. Inside the inner safe sits a letter from the Prime Minister. It tells us what we must do in the event of a nuclear attack on the United Kingdom.

If this ever happened, we'd receive a coded message. I would rush through the boat to the control room carrying the message. I would hold it above my head so another officer who follows me can see it. He makes sure that I don't swap the message for one that I've created myself.

In the control room, the Captain and myself would open the safes together. We each have one half of the combination. We'd be joined by the WEO (Weapons Engineering Officer). Together, we would decode the message using **cryptographic codes** that are stored alongside the Prime Minister's letter. All three of us have to agree that the message we received precisely matches the codes.

The Captain would then order me to bring the submarine to action stations. The Captain would take his place in the control room. The WEO would go to the missile center from where he would actually fire the missiles. The missile trigger is in the handle of a Colt 45 pistol.

The Captain would say, "The WEO has my permission to fire."

That's it. The WEO would click the trigger and release the most devastating weapon ever devised. Once you heard that click, you would know that you're no more than 30 minutes from the end of the world. It's a sobering thought."

IT'S A FACT!

The Royal Navy of the United Kingdom currently has 89 ships in service. These include SSNs (attack submarines), SSBNs (ballistic missile submarines), aircraft carriers, a helicopter carrier, frigates (small warships), and patrol vessels.

The United States Navy operates over 280 ships and submarines. It is the largest navy in the world.

Submarines are painted black to help them hide. The color black has proven to be most effective at hiding the submarine in the ocean below shallow depths.

Members of the crew of an SSBN are not allowed contact with their families when at sea. This is in case such contact gives their position away. Only the Captain and XO will know the submarine's location.

A typical United States Navy SSN crew consists of 14 Officers, 18 Chief Petty Officers (senior crew members), and 109 other crew members. The crew of an SSBN normally numbers 150.

Nuclear Submariners online
www.navy.mil/navydata/fact_display.asp?cid=4100&tid=100&ct=4
www.royalnavy.mod.uk/operations-and-support/submarine-service/
http://science.howstuffworks.com/submarine.htm

GLOSSARY

atom A basic unit of matter consisting of a dense, central nucleus surrounded by a cloud of negatively charged electrons. A source of nuclear energy

ballistic missile A missile that delivers a warhead (often nuclear) to a predetermined target

carbon dioxide (CO_2) A colorless, odorless gas present in the atmosphere and formed during breathing

cruise missile A missile that acts somewhat like a pilotless plane. It has a powerful guidance system and can hit precise targets from a great distance. Cruise missiles can be fired from submarines or warships. They can be fitted with nuclear warheads

cryptographic codes Secret codes that cannot be understood if they are intercepted by an enemy

mine An explosive device that can be detonated by touching it, by being close to it, or by a fuse on a timer

nuclear deterrent A nuclear weapon held by one country to discourage nuclear attacks by other countries

nuclear fission A nuclear reaction in which the nucleus of an atom splits into smaller parts, generating immense heat

nuclear reactor A device in which nuclear chain reactions (a series of reactions) are started, controlled, and sustained at a steady rate

radiation (nuclear) Harmful form of radiation given off by nuclear material. Exposure to nuclear radiation can cause skin burns and, at high levels, cancers and other tumors

radioactive Something that is emitting radiation, either directly from unstable atomic nuclei, or because of a nuclear reaction

special forces Highly trained military units, such as the Green Berets and Navy SEALs (Sea Air and Land forces), that conduct special operations

subatomic Smaller than, or found within, an atom

torpedo A self-propelled underwater missile launched from a tube located inside the hull of a submarine or warship

Trident D5 nuclear missiles A submarine-launched ballistic missile. A Trident D5 can have multiple nuclear warheads that can be targeted to different places. The missiles can be accurately targeted to within a few feet. The United Kingdom and United States both have Trident D5s

INDEX

Printed in the USA—

HOTEL SPACES

MONTSE BORRÀS

BEVERLY MASSACHUSETTS

ROCKPORT PUBLISHERS

Copyright © 2008 by LOFT Publications

First published in the United States of America by
Rockport Publishers, a member of
Quayside Publishing Group
100 Cummings Center
Suite 406-L
Beverly, MA 01915
Telephone: (978) 282-9590
Fax: (978) 283-2742
www.rockpub.com

ISBN-13: 978-1-59253-432-6
ISBN-10: 1-59253-432-5

Editorial coordination:
Catherine Collin

Editor and texts:
Montse Borràs

Translation:
Heather Bagott

Art director:
Mireia Casanovas Soley

Layout:
Anabel Naranjo

Cover Image:
Mondrian Scottsdale, © Morgans Hotel Group

Editorial project:
LOFT Publications
Via Laietana, 32, 4° of. 92
08003 Barcelona, Spain
Tel.: 0034 932 688 088
Fax: 0034 932 687 073
e-mail: loft@loftpublications.com
www.loftpublications.com

Printed in China

Contents

Introduction >

Some of the earliest known tourists were the pilgrims of the Middle Ages, who travelled across Europe for religious and mystical reasons. *The Canterbury Tales*, written at the end of the fourteenth century, was the first literary offering about voluntary travel in the Western world.

But, journeys relating to health have existed since time immemorial. In the *Odyssey*, Ulysses talks of the pleasures of thermal bathing. Hippocrates considered water, healthy living, light, a good diet, and peace of mind as curatives for the body. The reasons that millions of people travel every year on vacation remain the same.

Today there are few paradises left to discover so new havens need to be created: special places that take travelers into the realm of fantasy. Hotels become destinations in themselves, just as much in big cities as they do in exclusive retreats far away from tourist and commercial activity. Prestigious designers and artists are given carte blanche to create unique spaces in boutique hotels, where every room is its own universe.

Trends are blended together with astonishing results, and the possibilities are endless: minimalism with elements of Mexican folklore, high tech fused with new baroque, and renaissance ambience in the heart of the urban jungle.

Some of the most original and spectacular hotels from every corner of the world are assembled here. Located in large cities or far away paradises, the hotels included are authentic style gems, created for the pleasure and relaxation of the contemporary traveller, whose travels to new and exciting places allow an exploration of the inner self.

Façades >

Façades and exterior spaces function as business cards for hotels. They give us an idea of what lies behind them. Sometimes these first impressions are faithful to what is to be found inside; other times they playfully highlight the contrasts. The exteriors of the hotels displayed in this chapter have been created or restored with the aim of establishing an intimate dialogue with the spaces they house.

Today, guests wish to feel that they not only stay at a particular hotel but that they live there, if only for one night. Consequently, the hotel should give an impression that starts from the very moment guests approach it. During the last few years, it has become a real challenge for architects and designers to impress the visitor who has already set foot in the major cities of the world.

From the architectural point of view, a hotel can be the means by which to defy the aesthetic uniformity that plagues the design of today's public places. The quest, to conform to an often misunderstood ideal of modernity, has spawned a generation of dismal clones all over the planet. This chapter shows how tradition, technology, or simply vernacular forms can challenge this dreary burden of preconceived ideas that currently afflicts the hotel industry.

> Indigo Hotel | © Cristóbal Palma

> Uma Paro Bhutan | © Uma Paro Hotels

> Hospes Palacio de los Patos | © Hospes Hotels & Moments

> Casa Tritón | © Casa Tritón

> Cavas Wine Lodge | © Virginia del Giudice

> Hotel Azúcar | © Undine Prohl

> W Retreat & Spa Maldives | © W Hotels

> Hotel Marqués de Riscal | © Adrian Tyler

> Byblos Art Hotel Villa Amistà | © Byblos Art Hotel Villa Amistà

> Sixty Hotel Riccione | © Yael Pincus

> Sant Cugat Hotel | © Raimon Solà

> Gramercy Park Hotel | © Ian Schrager Hotels

> Hotel Hesperia Tower | © Jordi Llorella

> Mykonos Theoxenia | © Design Hotels

> Kasbah Tamadot | © Virgin Limited Edition

> Burj Al Arab | © Jumeirah Hotels

Pools & Terraces >

In most ancient cultures, water was considered a gift from the gods. The Egyptians, the Assyrians, and even the Romans understood the splendor that water bestowed upon gardens and landscapes. Later civilizations continued to enjoy thermal baths and the play of water. Today pools have infinite possibilities. Inspired by nature or by tradition, set in the architectural structure that surrounds them, their beauty seems to merge with the sky and sea, recalling the magical, ever-changing spectacle of water.

This chapter is dedicated to hotel pools and other uses of water, such as spas and fitness spaces, and to those areas directly influenced by them: terraces, solariums, outside lounges, etc. They provide the perfect setting for unwinding. Pools and spas are great incentives for those who wish to pamper themselves with special treatments or simply enjoy the marvellous sensations of the sun and water. These spaces are the icing on the cake of each hotel; they enhance the splendor of the place and establish a dialog with their natural or urban setting, while creating a relaxing and calm atmosphere.

> Casa Tritón | © Casa Tritón

> Casa Tritón | © Casa Tritón

> Byblos Art Hotel Villa Amistà | © Byblos Art Hotel Villa Amistà

> Delano Hotel | © Morgans Hotel Group

> Hotel Azúcar | © Undine Prohl

> Hospes Palacio de los Patos | © Adrià Goula

> Mondrian Scottsdale | © Morgans Hotel Group

> Mykonos Theoxenia | © Design Hotels

> Burj Al Arab | © Jumeirah Hotels

> Byblos Art Hotel Villa Amistà | © Byblos Art Hotel Villa Amistà

> Kasbah Tamadot | © Virgin Limited Edition

> Hotel Marqués de Riscal | © Adrian Tyler

> W Retreat & Spa Maldives | © W Hotels

> Cavas Wine Lodge | © Virginia del Giudice

> Indigo Hotel | © Cristóbal Palma

Lobbies & Lounges >

Until recently, hotel communal areas have been quite undervalued. The look and decoration of the bedrooms and service areas were always given greater importance than those of the lounges and lobbies. However, designers and architects are beginning to focus more on these spaces, which, in addition to offering immense creative possibilities, contribute to forming the overall atmosphere and the real backbone of establishments. They are becoming places in which to see and be seen, to meet and chat, and—most importantly—to welcome new guests.

Hoteliers have recognized that ongoing changes in society's tastes and needs call for a live-or-die approach to hotel service as a priority. Lobbies and lounges can host social events and merge interior and exterior spaces while conferring their hotels with unique flair and atmosphere. From a rich, calm, baroque style to a fresh, luminous, and simple look—and everything in between—these areas are real windows into the character of the hotel and the style statement made by the owners and designers.

> W Mexico City | © Studio Gaia

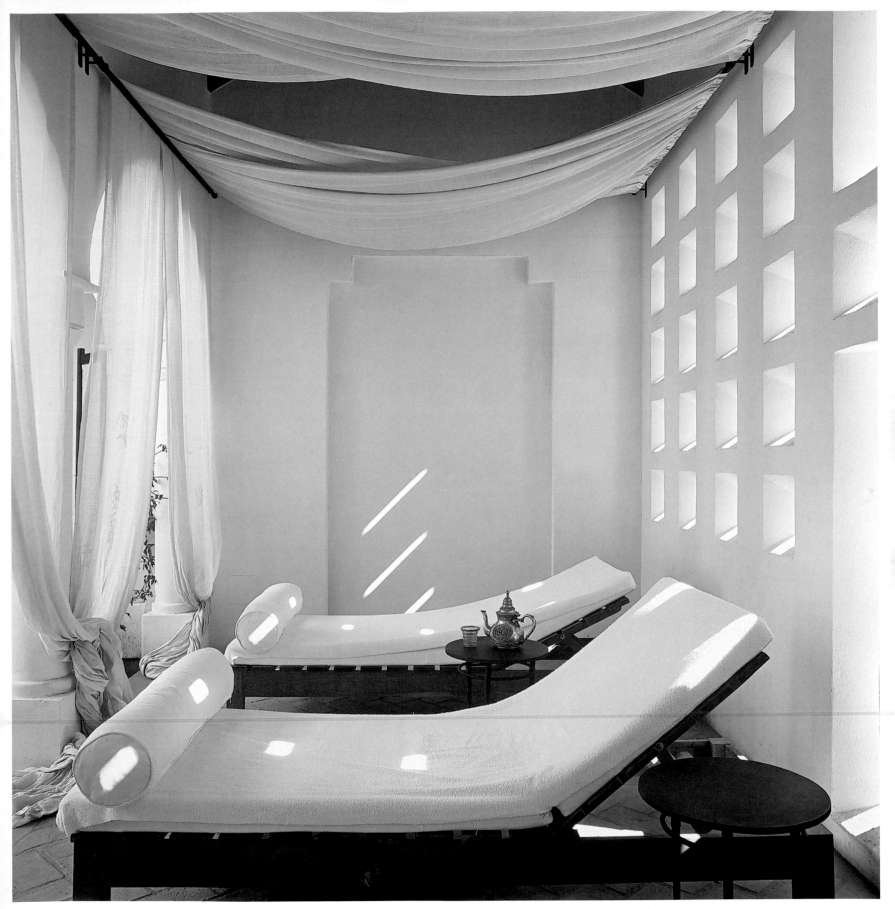

> Cavas Wine Lodge | © Virginia del Giudice

> Hotel Fox | © Hotel Fox

> Hotel Hesperia Tower | © Jordi Llorella

> Indigo Hotel | © Cristóbal Palma

> Chic & Basic Born | © Rafael Vargas/Chic & Basic

> Hotel Lutecia | © Fernando Guerra | FG + SG Fotografia de Arquitectura

> Sixty Hotel Riccione | © Yael Pincus

> Hotel Azúcar | © Undine Prohl

> W Retreat & Spa Maldives | © W Hotels

> Bulgari Hotels & Resorts Bali | © Bulgari Hotels & Resorts

> The G Hotel Galway | © Luke White

> Haymarket Hotel | © Design Hotels

> The G Hotel Galway | © Luke White

> Byblos Art Hotel Villa Amistà | © Byblos Art Hotel Villa Amistà

> Gramercy Park Hotel | © Ian Schrager Hotels

> Hospes Palacio de los Patos | © Adrià Goula

> Burj Al Arab | © Jumeirah Hotel

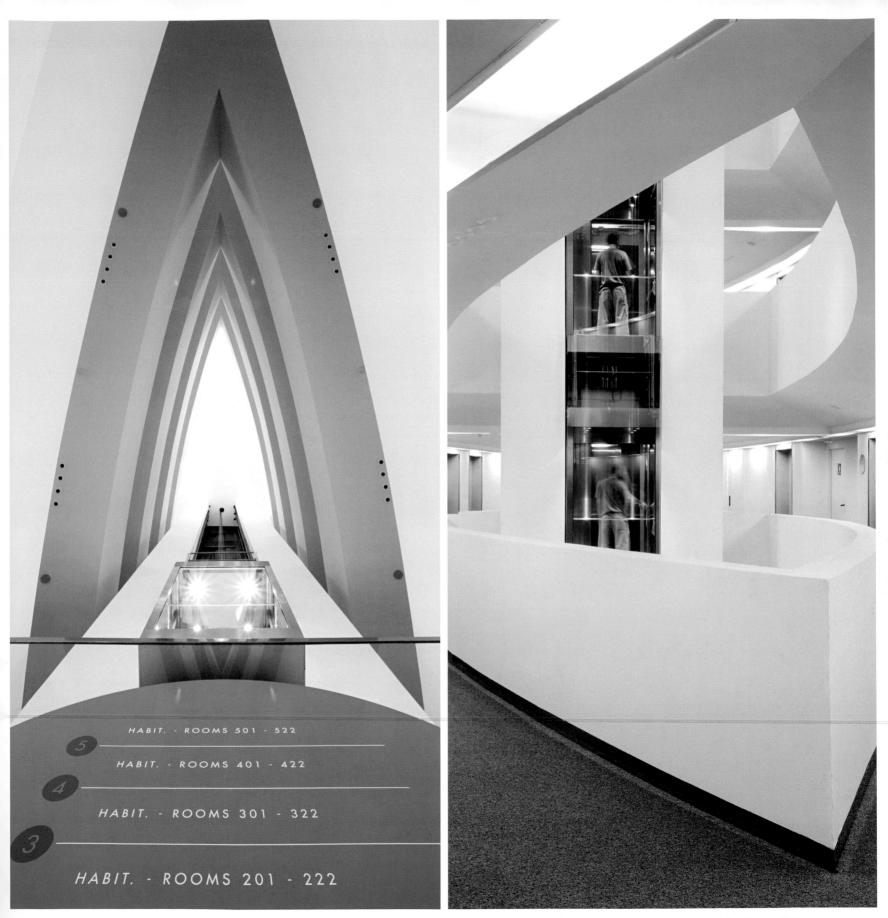

HABIT. - ROOMS 501 - 522

HABIT. - ROOMS 401 - 422

HABIT. - ROOMS 301 - 322

HABIT. - ROOMS 201 - 222

> Sant Cugat Hotel | © Raimon Solà

> Delano Hotel | © Morgans Hotel Group

> Mondrian Scottsdale | © Morgans Hotel Group

> Mondrian Scottsdale | © Morgans Hotel Group

> Kasbah Tamadot | © Virgin Limited Edition

> Uma Paro Bhutan | © Uma Paro Hotels

> Lloyd Hotel | © Lloyd Hotel

Bars & Restaurants >

One of the main functions of the new generation of hotels is to offer a unique dining experience. World-famous chefs are opening restaurants in the most exclusive hotels, offering a range of different styles and variations of cuisine. In big cities, the bars and cocktail lounges of hotels have become the hippest and most sophisticated meeting places. This is why the service areas require a distinctive style, in harmony with the atmosphere of the place for which they have been created. In this sense, the concept of luxury is continually evolving: it no longer means providing ostentatious spaces, full of glitz and chandeliers. Today's visitors want to feel unique simply because of where they are staying, which means that luxury is a matter of finding that sought-after difference.

Every detail enhances the character of these spaces: the lights provide different atmospheres; the colors and textures of the materials convey suitable feelings. The bars and restaurants featured in this chapter are evidence of the variety of possibilities that modern hotels have to offer.

> W Mexico City | © W Hotels

> Paradise Hotel Busan | © Studio Gaia

> Hotel Fox | © Hotel Fox

> The G Hotel Galway | © Luke White

> Hotel Hesperia Tower | © Jordi Llorella

> Indigo Hotel | © Cristóbal Palma

> W Retreat & Spa Maldives | © W Hotels

> Hotel Marqués de Riscal | © Adrian Tyler

> Byblos Art Hotel Villa Amistà | © Byblos Art Hotel Villa Amistà

> Gramercy Park Hotel | © Ian Schrager Hotels

> Chic & Basic Born | © Rafael Vargas/Chic & Basic

> Uma Paro Bhutan | © Uma Paro Hotels

> Burj Al Arab | © Jumeirah Hotels

> Sant Cugat Hotel | © Raimon Solà

> Hotel Lutecia | © Fernando Guerra | FG+SG Fotografia de Arquitectura

> Delano Hotel | © Morgans Hotel Group

> Mondrian Scottdale | © Morgans Hotel Group

> Mondrian Scottsdale | © Morgans Hotel Group

> Kasbah Tamadot | © Virgin Limited Edition

> Hotel du Petit Moulin | © Hotel du Petit Moulin

> Mykonos Theoxenia | © Design Hotels

Suites & Bedrooms >

The intimacy of a bedroom represents the zenith of a trip. The destination has been reached, the journey is over, and it is time to relax and give way to adventure. The impersonal places of yesteryear have been converted into small universes where each detail has been conceived in a way that makes it possible to book the perfect space for each individual and allow the imagination to flow.

The luxury here doesn't come from just the exclusive amenities, but from distinct, unique design. In several cases, hotels have commissioned well-known artists to design each room, thus transforming their neutral spaces into individual stories. After a long hectic day in New York City, it is an extraordinary experience to feel transported to the early Renaissance in Flanders, or to sleep in a log cabin when visiting Amsterdam, not to mention waking up with a view of ancient windmills on top of a soft hill in Greece, or stepping out of bed on the Indian Sea's turquoise waters, which run under the glass floor of your bungalow in Maldives. This chapter showcases hotel bedrooms, born out of the wishes of a new generation of sophisticated global consumers and the talent of great designers and hotel entrepreneurs.

> Casa Tritón | © Casa Tritón

> Cavas Wine Lodge | © Virginia del Giudice

> The Grove | © Carlos Domínguez

> W Mexico City | © Studio Gaia

> Delano Hotel | © Morgans Hotel Group

> Hotel Azúcar | © Undine Prohl

> Sixty Hotel Riccione | © Yael Pincus

Someone was killed in this room

> Lloyd Hotel | © Lloyd Hotel

> Hotel Fox | © Hotel Fox

> Indigo Hotel | © Cristóbal Palma

> Hotel Fox | © Hotel Fox

> Chic & Basic Born | © Rafael Vargas/Chic & Basic

> Bulgari Hotels & Resorts Bali | © Bulgari Hotels & Resorts

> Bulgari Hotels & Resorts Bali | © Bulgari Hotels & Resorts

> Hotel Marqués de Riscal | © Adrian Tyler

> W Retreat & Spa Maldives | © W Hotels

> Uma Paro Bhutan | © Uma Paro Hotels

> Hospes Palacio de los Patos | © Hospes Hotels & Moments

> Gramercy Park Hotel | © Ian Schrager Hotels

> Byblos Art Hotel Villa Amistà | © Byblos Art Hotel Villa Amistà

> Hospes Palacio de los Patos | © Hospes Hotels & Moments

> Delano Hotel | © Morgans Hotel Group

> Kasbah Tamadot | © Virgin Limited Edition

> Hotel du Petit Moulin | © Hotel du Petit Moulin

> Hotel du Petit Moulin | © Hotel du Petit Moulin

> Mykonos Theoxenia | © Design Hotels

> Mykonos Theoxenia | © Design Hotels

Directory

Bulgari Hotels & Resorts Bali
Banjar Dinas Kangin
Uluwatu, 80368 Bali, Indonesia
P: +62 361 847 1000
www.bulgarihotels.com
Designers: Antonio Citterio & Partners

Burj Al Arab (Jumeriah Hotels)
PO Box 73137, Dubai
P: +97 143 665 000
www.jumeirah.com
Designers: Atkins Design

Byblos Art Hotel Villa Amistà
Via Cedrare, 78, Corrubbio di Negarine
37029 Verona, Italy
P: +39 045 685 5555
www.byblosarthotel.com
Designers: Alessandro Mendini, Dino Facchini

Casa Tritón
Careyes, Mexico
P: +1 817 735 9629
www.casatriton.com
Arquitecto: Marco Aldaco

Cavas Wine Lodge
Costaflores s/n, Alto Agrelo
5507 Mendoza, Argentina
P: +54 (0)261 410 6927/28
www.cavaswinelodge.com
Architects: Pondal & Malencini
Designers: Teresa Giustinian, Felicitas Bermúdez

Chic & Basic Born (Chic & Basic)
Princesa, 50
08003 Barcelona, Spain
P: +34 932 954 652
www.chicandbasic.com
Architects: Xavier Claramunt

Delano Hotel (Morgans Hotel Group)
1685 Collins Avenue
Miami Beach, FL 33139, USA
P: +1 305 672 2000
www.delano-hotel.com
Designers: Benjamin Noriega-Ortiz

Gramercy Park Hotel (Ian Schrager Hotels)
2 Lexington Avenue
New York, NY 10010, USA
P: +1 212 920 3300
www.gramercyparkhotel.com
Designers: Michael Overington, Anda Andrei

Haymarket Hotel (Firmdale Hotels)
1 Suffolk Place
London SW1Y 4BP, United Kingdom
P: +44 20 7470 4000
www.haymarkethotel.com
Designers: Tim & Kit Kemp

Hospes Palacio de los Patos (Hospes Hotels and Moments)
Solarillo de Gracia, 1
18002 Granada, Spain
P: +34 958 535 790
www.hospes.es
Designers: Xavier Claramunt, Martín Izquierdo

Hotel Azúcar
Carretera federal Nautla-Poza Rica, km 83.5
Monte Gordo, ZP 93588 Veracruz, Mexico
P: +232 321 0678/321 0804
www.hotelazucar.com
Designers: Carlos Couturier, Elias Adam, José Robredo

Hotel du Petit Moulin
29/31 rue du Poitou
75003 Paris, France
P: +33 142 74 1010
www.paris-hotel-petitmoulin.com
Designers: Christian Lacroix

Hotel Fox
Jarmerds Plads 3
DK-1551 Copenhagen V, Denmark
P: +45 33 13 3000
www.hotelfox.dk
Designers: Various artists

Hotel Hesperia Tower
Gran Via, 144
08907 Barcelona, Spain
P: +34 934 135 000
www.hesperiatower.es
Architects: Richard Rogers, Alonso & Balaguer

Hotel Lutécia
Av. Frei Miguel Contreiras, 52
1749-086 Lisboa, Portugal
+351 218 411 300
www.luteciahotel.com
Architects: FFCB Arquitectos

Hotel Marqués de Riscal
Torrea, 1
01340 Elciego (Álava), Spain
P: +34 945 180 888
www.marquesderiscal.com
Architects: Frank Gehry

Indigo Hotel
Ladrilleros, 105
Puerto Natales, Chile
P: +56 6141 3609
www.indigopatagonia.com
Architects: Sebastián Irarrazaval

Kasbah Tamadot (Virgin Limited Edition)
BP 67, 042150 Asni
Marrakech, Morocco
P: +212 (0) 2436 8200
www.virginlimitededition.com/kasbah
Designers: Virgin Limited Edition Design Team

Lloyd Hotel & Cultural Embassy
Oostelijke Handelskade 34
1019 BN Amsterdam, The Netherlands
P: +31 (0)20 561 3636
www.lloydhotel.com
Designers: Various artists

Mondrian Scottsdale (Morgans Hotel Group)
7353 East Indian School Road
Scottsdale, AZ 85251, USA
P: +1 480 308 1000
www.mondrianscottsdale.com
Designers: Benjamin Noriega-Ortiz

Mykonos Theoxenia (Design Hotels)
84600 Kato Mill
Mykonos, Greece
P: +30 228 902 2230
www.mykonostheoxenia.com
Designers: Yiannis Tsimas, Angelos Angelopoulos

Paradise Hotel Busan
Jung-dong, Haeundae-gu
Busan 612-846, Korea
P: +82 51 742 2121
http://busan.paradisehotel.co.kr
Designers: Studio Gaia

Sant Cugat Hotel (Habitat Hotels)
César Martinell, 2
08190 Sant Cugat del Vallès, Spain
P: +34 935 441 447
www.hotel-santcugat.com
Architects: BST Arquitectes
Designers: Sebas Bonet, Cesc Solà/La Creativa

Sixty Hotel Riccione (Sixty Group)
Via Milano 54
Riccione, Italy
P: +39 0541 697 851
www.sixtyhotel.com
Designers: Wichy Hassan/Sixty Group Design Team

The G Hotel Galway (Monogram Hotels)
Wellpark, Co Galway, Ireland
P: +353 (0)91 865 200
www.theghotel.ie/g/
Designers: Philip Treacy

The Grove
Chandler's Cross, Hertfordshire
WD3 4TG United Kingdom
www.thegrove.co.uk
P: +44 19 2380 7807
Architects: Scott & Brownrigg

Uma Paro Bhutan (Como Hotels & Resorts)
Paro, Bhutan
P: +975 8 271 597
www.uma.como.bz/paro
Designers: Como Group Design Team

W Retreat & Spa Maldives (Starwood Hotels)
Fesdu Island
North Ari Atoll, Maldives
P: +960 666 2222
www.starwoodhotels.com
Designers: Starwood Hotels Design Team

W Mexico City
Campos Elíseos 252 Chapultepec, Polanco
11560 Mexico City, Mexico
P: +52 (55) 9138 1800
www.starwoodhotels.com
Designers: Studio Gaia